MW01236025

AWESOME ATHLETES

KOBE BRYANT

Lydia Pyle

ABDO Publishing Company

visit us at
www.abdopub.com

Published by ABDO Publishing Company, 4940 Viking Drive, Edina, Minnesota 55435.
Copyright © 2004 by Abdo Consulting Group, Inc. International copyrights reserved in all
countries. No part of this book may be reproduced in any form without written permission from
the publisher.

Printed in the United States.

Cover Photo: *Sports Illustrated*
Interior Photos: Corbis pp. 23, 27, 29, 31; *Sports Illustrated* pp. 5, 9, 11, 13, 14, 15, 17, 19, 25

Editors: Tamara L. Britton and Jessica A. Klein
Art Direction: Neil Klinepier

Library of Congress Cataloging-in-Publication Data

Pyle, Lydia, 1972-
    Kobe Bryant / Lydia Pyle.
      p. cm. -- (Awesome athletes)
    Includes index.
    Summary: Looks at the personal life and professional basketball career of NBA star Kobe
Bryant of the Los Angeles Lakers.
    ISBN 1-59197-488-7
    1. Bryant, Kobe, 1978---Juvenile literature. 2. Basketball players--United States--Biography--
Juvenile literature. [1. Bryant, Kobe, 1978- 2. Basketball players. 3. African Americans--
Biography.] I. Title. II. Series.

GV884.B794P95 2003
796.323'092--dc21
[B]
                               2003045356

Cumberland County Public Library
  & Information Center
Hope Mills Branch
3411 Golfview Drive
Hope Mills, NC 28348

Contents

Kobe Bryant

Kobe Bryant is becoming an unforgettable player in the **National Basketball Association (NBA)**. His seven-year career has had its ups and downs. But, Kobe has proven that going into the NBA right out of high school can be done. He has not only done it, but he has done it well.

When Kobe entered the NBA, he was the youngest player in the league's history at 18 years, 2 months, and 11 days. This was two months younger than Stanley Brown, who did it in 1947. Kobe held this record until Jermaine O'Neal entered the NBA at 18 years, 1 month, and 22 days.

Since he began his career with the Los Angeles Lakers in 1996, Kobe has acquired a long list of accomplishments. In 1997, he won the Nestle Crunch Slam Dunk contest and became the youngest player to start in an NBA game.

Kobe has been selected to play in the NBA All-Star Game five times. His team has won three **consecutive** national championships. Kobe's talent, hard work, and determination have gotten him to where he is today—an NBA star!

Jim McIlvaine puts a mid-air stop to Kobe's drive to the hoop.

Life in Italy

Kobe Bryant was born on August 23, 1978, in Philadelphia, Pennsylvania. He is the third child of Joe and Pamela Bryant. Kobe has two older sisters, Sharia and Shaya.

Basketball was a big part of the Bryant household. Kobe's father Joe, known as Jellybean, played in the **NBA** for eight seasons. When Kobe saw his father playing basketball on television, Kobe imitated him by playing with his miniature basketball hoop.

When there was a time-out in the game on television, Kobe would take a time-out from playing, too. When his father wiped his face with a towel, Kobe would do the same.

But, basketball wasn't the only thing going on in the Bryant household. Kobe's parents made it very clear to their children that education and family values were also an important part of life.

In 1984, when Kobe was six years old, his dad's career moved the family to Rieti, Italy. The move was not easy for Kobe and his sisters, especially since they didn't speak Italian. But they quickly learned the language by getting together after school and teaching each other the new words they had learned.

The Bryant family frequently moved from one town to the next during their eight-year stay in Europe. This made it hard for Kobe and his sisters to make friends. The Bryant family relied on each other for friendship and company. They became very close.

Kobe's father quickly became a basketball star in Italy. Kobe attended many of his father's games and even hung out at some of his practices. **Professional** basketball was much more laid-back in Italy than in America. Sometimes Kobe was allowed to shoot baskets during halftime at his father's games. Kobe would later recall, "The crowd would be cheering me on. I loved it."

Kobe's grandparents often sent videotapes of **NBA** games to Italy. Kobe watched them over and over. He studied moves and plays and especially loved watching tapes of Los Angeles Lakers star Magic Johnson.

Kobe's love for the game grew each day. But, this passion was not something that other children in Italy shared with Kobe. "After school I would be the only guy on the basketball court, working on my moves, and then kids would start showing up with their soccer ball," Kobe remembers. "It was either go home or be the goalkeeper."

Returning to America

When Kobe was 14, his family returned to the United States and moved to the Philadelphia suburb of Wynnewood. Kobe entered the eighth grade at Bala Cynwyd Junior High School.

Moving back to the United States was not easy for Kobe. The United States was very different from Europe. And now Kobe did not speak English well. Kobe was unfamiliar with most things that children his age were into, such as television shows and music groups. Kobe had a hard time making friends and fitting in.

So Kobe continued to concentrate on his basketball skills. He played for his eighth-grade team and was a standout. Lower Merion High School basketball coach Gregg Downer heard about Kobe and wanted to see him in action. Downer invited Kobe to join his varsity team for a practice. After watching Kobe for a few minutes the coach said, "This kid's going to be a pro."

Sixers's center Todd MacCulloch is no match as Kobe drives for the dunk.

High School Years

Kobe attended Lower Merion High School in Ardmore, Pennsylvania. He made the varsity team his freshman year. He was a starter and averaged 18 points per game. His ability to dribble, shoot, and rebound caught everyone's attention.

Kobe practiced hard and played even harder. He was dedicated to becoming the best basketball player he could be. "He is blessed with a lot of natural ability and great genes, but the work ethic is his and it's very strong," said Downer of Kobe.

At the end of his freshman season, Kobe told a friend that he wanted to play in the **NBA**. Not only did he want to play in the NBA, but he also wanted to play right out of high school.

Over the next three years, Kobe worked hard during the season and also during the summer months. He played in many different summer leagues and steadily improved his game.

Opposite page: Kobe wore number 33 for Lower Merion High School.

During Kobe's senior year, he led his team to the Pennsylvania AAAA state championship. He averaged 31 points, 12 rebounds, 7 assists, 4 blocks, and 5 steals per game. Kobe finished his high school career as the all-time leading scorer in southern Pennsylvania high school history with 2,883 points.

Kobe was named to the McDonald's All-American Team in 1996. That same year, he was named National Player of the Year by *USA Today* and *Parade* magazine. Kobe continued to earn awards in 1996, when he was named Naismith Player of the Year and Gatorade Circle of Champions High School Player of the Year.

Besides being an excellent basketball player, Kobe was also a solid B-average student and scored well on the SAT. He was the perfect candidate for a college basketball **scholarship**. Many well-known colleges such as Duke, Michigan, and North Carolina were hoping that Kobe would accept a scholarship from them.

In every city the Lakers play young fans rush to meet Kobe!

THE MAKING OF AN AWESOME ATHLETE

Kobe is one of the best players in the NBA today.

1978	1984	1993	1996
Born August 23 in Philadelphia, Pennsylvania	Moves to Italy with his family	Returns to America	Becomes southern Pennsylvania's all-time leading scorer with 2,88 points

How Awesome Is He?

Kobe is the youngest player in NBA history to reach 10,000 points for his career. See how he compares to others who have reached this milestone.

Player	Age
Kareem Abdul-Jabbar	25 years, 344 days
Shareef Abdur-Rahim	26 years, 17 days
Kobe Bryant	**24 years, 193 days**
Michael Jordan	25 years, 343 days
Bob McAdoo	25 years, 148 days
Shaquille O'Neal	25 years, 341 days

KOBE BRYANT

TEAM: LOS ANGELES LAKERS
NUMBER: 8
POSITION: GUARD
HEIGHT: 6 FEET, 7 INCHES
WEIGHT: 220 POUNDS

1996

oins the Lakers
nd becomes the
oungest player
ever join the
BA

1998

Youngest player
to ever start an
NBA All-Star
Game

2000

Named to All-
Defensive first
team and All-NBA
second team

2003

Youngest player
in NBA history to
reach 10,000
points

- Scored all-time career high of 56 points on January 14, 2002
- Made 12 three-pointers on January 7, 2003, setting a new NBA record
- Scored more than 40 points in nine consecutive games February 6-23, 2003
- Became youngest player in NBA history to score 10,000 points on March 5, 2003

Highlights

The Decision

The anticipation of Kobe Bryant's decision about his future was growing daily. "I don't think there's a wrong choice, either way you look at it," Kobe said about his choice to attend college or go directly into the **NBA**.

Many people believed that Kobe would be making a bad decision if he went into the NBA without playing college ball. Not many players had made it in the NBA without going to college first.

But Kobe did have support for going directly into the NBA. Some people felt his maturity and background were much different than most high school seniors. Kobe's parents thought it was his choice.

On April 29, 1996, Kobe held a press conference in the gym of Lower Merion. Television cameras and reporters from all over the country were present. When the bell rang at 2:25, signaling the end of classes, students filled the gym. Kobe walked in and announced, "I have decided to skip college and take my talent to the NBA." The crowd erupted with cheers, and Kobe flashed his bright smile. "Playing in the NBA has been my dream since I was three," Kobe said.

Kobe penetrates to the basket and kicks the ball out in a game against the Houston Rockets.

Laker-Bound

The **NBA draft** was just two months away. Many teams were interested in Kobe, but were not sure if they were willing to gamble on such a young player. Several teams, including the New Jersey Nets and the Los Angeles Lakers, had Kobe work out with them to see his skills in person.

Jerry West, president of the Lakers said, "He was the most skilled player we've ever worked out, the kind of skill you don't see very often." West was convinced that the Lakers needed Kobe on their team.

But there was one problem. The Lakers had the 24th pick in the first round. They were sure that Kobe would be gone by the time their turn came to pick.

The day of the draft finally arrived. Kobe was nervous and was not sure what would happen. He was quite surprised when the Charlotte Hornets used their 13th pick to acquire him. He was the youngest player ever drafted into the NBA.

Kobe was quickly traded to the Los Angeles Lakers for center Vlade Divac. Kobe signed a three-year, $3.5

million deal
with the Lakers.
At the signing
ceremony Kobe
said, "It's a
dream come
true to come to
a team like L.A.
that has great
history. It was
a team I looked
up to growing
up." Kobe
packed up his
bags and moved
to Los Angeles,
California. His
mom, dad, and
sisters came
with him.

**Veteran Utah Jazz
guard John
Stockton tries to
keep Kobe in
check with
smothering
defense.**

New Kid on the Court

Kobe bought a six-bedroom house in Pacific Palisades, California. His family lived there with him. Kobe began to adjust to life in Los Angeles. He quickly signed **endorsements** with Adidas, Sprite, and Spalding.

Before training camp started, Kobe played pickup basketball in Venice Beach. In one of those games, Kobe fell and broke a bone in his left wrist. He was unable to start practicing with the team when training camp opened in October. He missed five weeks of camp.

Kobe attended practices and ran the drills, but could not catch, pass, dribble, or shoot the ball. But by the end of training camp, Kobe was able to join in with the team practices. He showed his teammates what he could do, and they nicknamed him "Showboat."

Kobe's first chance at playing in an **NBA** game came on November 3, 1996. The Lakers were playing their second game in the regular season against the Minnesota Timberwolves. Kobe became the youngest player to play an NBA game that night.

Kobe was invited to play in the Schick **Rookie** Game during the All-Star weekend. He put on a show! Kobe scored a record 31 points during the game and was named Most Valuable Player (MVP).

Kobe also showed his talent during the Nestle Crunch slam-dunk contest. The judges were wowed by Kobe's between-the-legs windmill dunk. He won the contest by scoring 49 out of 50 points.

In his first year with the team, the Lakers made the playoffs. In the second round against the Utah Jazz, Kobe took the game-winning shot, and threw an airball.

The game went into overtime, and Kobe tossed up three more airballs. The Lakers lost and were out of the playoffs. Kobe was disappointed but worked hard that summer to gear up for the next season.

Growing in the NBA

Kobe came ready to play when the 1997–98 season began. Although he was not in the starting lineup, Kobe got some good playing time. He began to show everyone his talent. People often compared Kobe's skills to those of Michael Jordan.

Kobe was voted to start in the All-Star Game and became the youngest player ever to be selected. The Lakers made it to the playoffs that year, but were defeated once again by the Utah Jazz. Kobe ended the season averaging 15.4 points per game.

The 1998–99 basketball season didn't begin until January 1999. The players' union contract had expired, and the season was delayed until a deal was worked out. That was just the beginning of the team's problems.

Differences between Kobe and teammate Shaquille O'Neal started to show, and the team struggled on the court. When the regular season ended, Kobe had averaged almost 20 points per game. The Lakers made it to the second round of the playoffs but were defeated by the San Antonio Spurs.

Miami Heat guard Eddie Jones battles Kobe for a key rebound.

Three-Time Champions

The Lakers knew they had the talent needed to win a championship, but they needed a leader to get them there. They found that in former Chicago Bulls coach Phil Jackson.

Kobe **thrived** during the 1999–2000 season under his new coach. Kobe had signed a six-year, $71 million contract with the Lakers and was committed to the team. His ability to play on a winning team was showing through.

Jackson helped Kobe and O'Neal learn to play together and not work against each other. The team clicked! The Lakers finished the regular season with a 67-15 record.

The Lakers made it to the finals in the playoffs and were playing the Indiana Pacers for the title. Kobe sprained his ankle during the second game of the playoffs and was unable to play the third game. But, the team pulled together and won the 2000 **NBA** championship in six games. Kobe scored 26 points in the last game.

Kobe was named to the All-Defensive first team and All-NBA second team in 2000. In May, Kobe announced that he was engaged to marry his girlfriend, Vanessa Laine.

Kobe and the Lakers came out ready to win another title in the 2000–01 season.

Shaq and Kobe celebrate their first championship after beating the Indiana Pacers in six games in the 2000 NBA finals.

But, they hit some bumps in the road, with every team coming to the games ready to beat the defending champions.

Kobe had his ups and downs during the season, scoring as many as 51 points in one game and less than 20 in others. But the Lakers won the title for the second straight year by beating the Philadelphia 76ers.

Could the Lakers three-peat? That was the question everyone was asking as the 2001–02 season began. To help achieve that goal, Kobe spent the summer working out and put on 15 pounds of muscle.

Kobe dazzled the crowds with his moves and averaged 25.5 points, 5.5 rebounds, and 5.5 assists per game during the season. Kobe scored his all-time career high of 56 points against the Memphis Grizzlies on January 14, 2002.

He also was awarded the MVP at the All-Star Game, his fifth. Kobe and his teammates were invited to the White House to meet President George W. Bush. Kobe presented the president with a Lakers team jersey. Later that year, the Lakers went on to win their third **consecutive NBA** title by sweeping the New Jersey Nets.

Opposite page: President Bush jokes with Kobe after receiving Lakers jersey number 1.

Kobe Today

Today, Kobe is one of the leading scorers in the **NBA**. On January 7, 2003, Kobe set a new record for three-pointers. He made 12 three-pointers in a game against the Seattle SuperSonics, nine of which were in a row. He scored 45 points in that game, and it gave the Lakers another win. "I mean, it wasn't like the basket was so huge, but it just felt like my rhythm was great," Kobe said about his shooting that night.

In one unforgettable streak in February, Kobe scored more than 40 points in nine **consecutive** games! The streak began with a 46-point spectacle against the New York Nicks on February 6. He ended with a 41-point performance on February 23 against the Seattle SuperSonics. Along the way, Kobe scored an incredible 52 points against Yao Ming and the Houston Rockets on February 18. And on March 5, Kobe became the youngest player in NBA history to score 10,000 points.

Kobe's personal life was also going well. He and Vanessa had welcomed a baby girl, Natalia, into their family on January 19. They also bought a new home in Newport Beach, California.

The Lakers started out hot in the 2003 playoffs. After beating the Minnesota Timberwolves in six games, the team moved to San Antonio to play the Spurs. But a fourth championship was not to be. The Spurs defeated the Lakers in six games.

It was a difficult loss, but Kobe isn't letting it slow him down. He will play in the 2004 summer Olympic Games in Athens, Greece. "It hit me one morning," Kobe said after agreeing to play in the Olympics. "I wanted to compete . . . and bring home what's rightfully ours."

Coach Jackson celebrates with Kobe and Shaq after besting the New Jersey Nets to win a third straight championship in June 2002.

Glossary

consecutive - following one after the other in order.

draft - an event during which NBA teams choose amateur players to play on their team.

endorsements - allowing a company to use your name and image to sell a product in exchange for money.

National Basketball Association (NBA) - a professional basketball league in the United States and Canada consisting of the Eastern and Western Conferences.

professional - working for money rather than pleasure.

rookie - a new player.

scholarship - a gift of money to help a student pay for instruction.

thrive - to do well.

Web Sites

To learn more about Kobe Bryant, visit ABDO Publishing Company on the World Wide Web at **www.abdopub.com**. Web sites about Kobe Bryant are featured on our Book Links page. These links are routinely monitored and updated to provide the most current information available.

Index